relaxing
in the bliss
of self-acceptance

fred andrle

spring night stars
the courage of light
in darkness

relaxing
in the bliss
of self-acceptance

haiku, senryu,
and small poems

fred andrle

2025

For Marlene

Copyright © 2025 Fred Andrle
All rights reserved

ISBN 978-1-880977-70-5

Published 2025
XOXOX Press, Gambier, OH 43022 USA

Book design by Jerry Kelly
Haiga illustrations by Marlene Hyman

Available to readers at local independent bookshops and on the web.

Booksellers, kindly order via Ingram catalog.

Library of Congress Control Number: 2024950354

spring rain
children leap
grownups crouch

lilting voices
in the hedgerow
sparrow cheer

deepest me

beyond

all thought's travail

deep night

the warehouse worker

breaks for lunch

call the dandelion
flower
an end to weeds

a pressure
on her knee
big dog's a leaner

whisk of wind
shiver of maple
spirit-talk

sitting
quietly sitting
my evening body

spring-wide sky
the grace
of soaring vultures

comedy
of mind-staged
tragedy

this tiny poem
this simple word:
peace

weary of fretting over
his life's elusive purpose
hot fudge sundae

winging, scuttling
marching, leaping
merry insect spring

thundersquall
the wrath
of loving couples

forgiving myself
for who I am
am not

hand in hand

we walk with life and death

this radiant moment

all the books
I'll never read
home library

spring orb spider
weaving
lethal loveliness

Canada goose day:
the pond, the grassy green
the pond and sleep

sun and shadow
we dwell
in both lights

party invite
introvert:
do they have a dog?

heedless humans
burning, howling
earth

suddenly
mimosa blossoms:
noticing my spring backyard

slumberous night

the calm

of deep acceptance

flocking, flowing

oak to maple

the poetry of starlings

her thoughts
like passing clouds
she's found her sun

target the drone
fire the missile
home for supper

birth to death
the courage
of our lives

spring dawn
me the chrysalis
yearning for flight

joy. grief
fear, calm
l'chaim!

muddy paws
of springtime hounds
my earthen jeans

all day rain
I pull up
the covers

gazing out

the narrow window

of belief

spring wind
bearing faint
the sound of battle

heaven-song
the melody
of stars

eighty years

her body

crowned in loveliness

fishing heron

still as morning

swift as sunlight

wishing

he could once more be

the child embracing wonder

daddy long legs

prince

of locomotion

forest walk
a pathway
through our grieving

eager spring
a soaring wind
I leap-sail skyward

time

a measurement

for moments unattended

spring dawn hues
the rainbow
of your voice

angelus bell
a calming
before nightfall

silent eyes
of housebound plants
observing marriage

spring morning light
my winter shadow
vanishes

he smiles at me
the neighbor dog
my morning anger fades

looking neither right nor left
nor up nor down
the calming

kissing her companion fear
goodbye
that marriage ended

sudden tears
my body
well of sorrow

tiny flier

mounts my notebook

I launch her with a breath

stillness of the room
beyond
my thought

tornado watch
the thrill
of grim arrivals

windy spring
he's breathing in
the dusts of peace and battle

morning dew
I share
your sunstruck fate

garden toad
the bliss
of steady presence

them

not me

the obituaries

here today

gone tomorrow

sing-songing our mortality

at last

the late moon rises

making the decision

battling

my inner critic

taking friendly fire

attending

the poetry reading:

near-death experience

all-day rain
the somnolence
of squirrels

single
mulberry leaf
the calling earth

stepping away
from endeavor
the serenity of idleness

wise fool
who placed the day
above ambition

clipping hair

listening calm

soul-barber

leaping, tumbling
glad, sad, glad
his cartwheeling moment

abandon thought
all ye
who'd enter bliss

crocodile

her ancient

sunny dreaming

rasping preacher
counterfeit
theology

pen in hand
I grant my spirit
voice

abandoning
the search
I peer within

spring morning calm
his heart
beats slow and surely

spring night stars
the courage of light
in darkness

deep spring rain
the calm
of dark descended

noontime drowse
the energy
of lassitude

hot dog vendor
relishing
the moment

chicken

on my dinner plate

all that suffering

raccoon stealth

the lure

of deep night mulberries

night moth
at my window
in lamplight, her golden eyes

poor me
one thought
too many

silence

of the earth

if we but listen

tears

beneath

an anger's eager thrust

famine, warfare, destitution

opening

our privileged morning mail

all-night slog
he wakes, he dreams
he bloody wakes

a single lamp
illumines night
lost highway

beyond the ceaseless conflict

beyond our turbulent thought

a stillness all around

pattering shower
sibilant oak
spring's delicate chorusing

spring thunderstorm
the powerful
seek shelter

spring river
all my ducks
in a row

spring rain
my brother's gravestone
washed clean

happy playground
greening park
everybody holy

humankind
the clash
of fear and spirit

spring moon and you
two lovely lights

feathers on the pathway

I whisper a prayer

for innocence

serenity

a cottonwood seed

drifting

silencing

our thought

to hear the day

spring wind my airy grievances

spring dusk stroll
amassing gnats
dizzy-fleet encircling

spring rain
a new leaf
opening

accepting

every grind, release

cherishing my moment

destiny's
chill wind
I hunker onward

rainy alley
rusting walker
death of an unknown neighbor

baying hounds

of spring backyards

earth's excitation

thunder's onslaught
lightning's spear
the great oak falls

spring geese
new goslings
innocent eyes

power of oak

whisper of maple

stillness of pine

robin's corpse

upon the lawn

the nonchalance of death

all the loving words

he never spoke

spring power walk
my anger
calms to grief

weary

of the burden

of my lifelong story

little wind

escorting

big spring rain

greening world
of happy spring
why must we die?

hissing clear
a twilight surge
summer's first cicadas

summer morning

peace

of sunlit soul

fallen redwood
even giants
pass

light, then dark
then light again
summer's reign of clouds

snake-green lawn
the soothing curl
of grasses

calm

before

desire's

storm

easeful winds

of sunny summer

my privileged ears and skin

close upon

our final breath

the great mystery

who would you wish
to hold your hand
as you lie dying?

summer haze
I peer at you
through my thoughts

we're partners

in creation

said the spider to the fly

serenity

of *no*, of every

beckoning solitude

after the battle

after the dying

a stillness of earth

shouting match

love's minor

imperfections

diving
into grief
deep healing waters

silent
summer moon
my gabbling thought

stink bug mounts

my summer window

her life, mine

wind that speaks
of many things
she listens by the door

final gift
my body
to the earth

wash clothes, mow lawn

trim nails, shave face

happy buddha day

frowning

in the glory

of the moment

strolling the summer

sunflower alley

heaven can wait

searching for a reason

to rise up

and make the bed

pleasance
of a morning
absent purpose

neighbor dog
licks my knee
joy of summer shorts

I whisper to my infant son
there's naught to fear
stone liar that I am

heaven-song

the melody

of stars

I want

I do not want

my killjoy mind

beyond, within

around us

love eternal

summer ease
I let what happens
happen

summer night
a calling owl
I answer, disrespectful

my brief life
I hope a polish
not a stain

summer snooze
I wake to wonder
who and why I am

hot summer lawn
sprinkler kids
cartwheeling

neighbor dog
licks his hand
somebody loves him

battling
my inner critic
taking friendly fire

summer dawn
the hums and clicks
of silence

one by one
the final sigh
of elders

cricket night
the summer meadow
sings

summer's blaze, I shelter
in the house
that conquered winter

searching
for a grace
within his sorrow

at the end

of the road

a new road beginning

insect, whale

the span

of soulful lives

I greet

an alley daffodil

haiku morning

summer lawn
the comfort
of familiar earth

amiable hog
beguiling cow
so sad: I kill you, eat you

resting

in the comfort

of your own loving-kindness

thought:
the mind's
autocracy

one robin
summer lawn
simple blessing

genial snakes

of summer lawns

joy-coiling

summer shade
the gentle arms
of oak

living
on the precipice
of dying

deep-night sleep
the instruction
of dreams

summer eve

she listens

to the harmony of gardens

elephants entrapped
the jailhouse
zoo

sorry
for your loss
those failing words

pleading with ants

to depart my summer kitchen

my reluctant broom

summer drone
of silken wings
the industry of insects

I hear his plaintive song
beyond the garden
summer's last cicada

listening

to the summer evening

cat and me

forgetting

who I told myself

I am

the old dog

said goodbye

departing in her arms

high-perched crow

his raucous thought

my summer morning grin

searing blaze
of summer mornings
shattered Earth rebels

summer heart
he opens wide
to caring

swiftly turns the summer day

I seek a meaning

in the vacuuming, the laundry

summer stroll
the heat
of words unspoken

eightieth year
an end
to youthful folly

wandering lost
in canyons
of her thought

I spin the day
from sad to glad
positioning presence

autumn age

a final chance

to cherish your aching self

autumn quiet
a neighbor's
solo cough

after-storm
the sigh
of quieting maples

all-day rain

the comfort

of afternoon blankets

thunderstorm

a pause

for predator, prey

death

a shrouding dark?

revealing light?

maple calm
before
a shouting wind

salmon entrée
once the dawning river
purling waters

autumn night
the stillness
of transience

steamrolled heart
the onslaught
of ambition

anxiety:

allowing ghosts

a presence

autumn ant making her way
across hills and valleys
of my comforter

twilight swallows
snatching
brief insects

brief-frisking squirrels

of temporal

backyards

garden fly
atop my knee
like me, you cast a shadow

calling children
big rain puddle
thunder afternoon

face to face

heart to heart

neighbor hound and me

joy beyond
the moment's
grief and shadow

far above
the raceway/freeway
steady autumn moon

life's wild ride
the bucking horse
of change

my mind
this smiling moment
happy marriage

sweet autumn hour
when first you feel
your life both kind and lovely

letting go:

the peace

of wish-less presence

book of life
the final chapter
kindness is the theme

old river rat
her autumn thoughts
her dreaming

filling the cup
lining the well
caring for me

autumn wind
salvific, brutal
tales I tell myself

demanding voices
fill my room
it's only me

autumn moon
the old dog
barks at shadows

drowsing through
my autumn life
careless mortal

autumn blue

a color

beyond leaf

strolling the lane
with my lifelong love
autumn leaf fall

we kill, we heal
we love, we hate
our tortuous humanity

torn between
service and dominion
political heart

autumn eve
a neighbor's long sigh
echoing

autumn gray
the comfort
of cloud and rain

breathing away

his fears and failures

morning meditation

canine smile, swing-time tail
a passing hound
gladdens my evening stroll

leaping cat
fleet butterfly
predation's merciless dance

seeking

never finding

the sparrow graveyard

beauty's allure
the chance arrangement
of a face

he complains
complains
but life won't budge

elder-years

a shadow

at the door

her life:

her troubled mind

her sacred heart

gone the many lives
the generations
only love remains

divorce
relief and grieving
happy heartbreak

autumn's last cricket call
the wistful beauty
of impermanence

rainy day
my body moist
and lengthening

autumn firefly
lonely
in the hedges

autumn dawn

I open my eyes

a new guilt arises

autumn's
drifting silences
she braids her twilight hair

he's got aches
she's got pains
the sigh of growing old

the moon

you see

the moon

you

desire

autumn twilight

sweethearts' stroll

dark lane by love emblazoned

the only cat
he ever loved
autumn backyard burial

autumn moon
he calms his thoughts
to silence

earnest robin

raucous crow

vigilant hawk

beery neighbor
slurred halloo
autumn night porch

fear:
the many haunts
of mind

I watch you

in the garden

we're together for a while

gravely ill

surprise

this time it's me

I never

heard a word

to comfort dying

waning moon
I glow content
with who I am, have been

pushing through
cascading griefs
soul stamina

empty chair
where sat a friend
departed

cardinal cheer
atop
the wounded maple

I'm bored with me
she merrily cried
let me tell you why

death's doorway/light's portal

old-guy walk
I stumble
down the block

back and forth
to and fro
the rhythm of ambivalence

autumn life

she begins to sense

an ending

soon you go

soon I go

our dear moments together

winter rain

my night bed

holds me close and warm

swiftly drops

a sodden snow

drear winter

rolling up
a snowman
boulder

hoping for
a winter sun
assertion

dark weave

of winter oaks

his chill confusion

kind he was
so gentle, he
memorial service

all the many souls
departed
fiftieth college reunion

life's stern embrace

the certainty

of loss

silence

of his darkened room

she's gone now

thought

despoiling

stillness

stilled and darkened
chill-enlightened
winter soul

parts and pieces
twisting strange
elder-body

frosting wind

departed sun

another bathrobe day

wedding dance
the virus
takes the floor

blood moon
we kiss
farewell

sleeping
like a winter bear
contented

library yells

the death

of whisper silence

departing America's
hiss and snarl
Canadian sunrise

young German Shepherd
looks at me, looks away
looks at me

forgotten dreams
tearing up
the old year calendar

winter midnight
slumbering couple
bedbug rodeo

verdant forest, arid plain
landscape
of my heart

searching for words

to pin the moment

haiku writer

yammer, yammer

guffaw, snort

the sounds of extroversion

deep-bone breath

I fall

into a quiet

ballot box

fear and hope

repository

winter stars
the clarity
of our fate

feeling blue
the day
I've painted gray

winter squirrel
digging up
breakfast

wounding words
I beg
my own forgiveness

climbing aboard
a thought train
rolling toward disaster

she releases thought
the night is quiet
the room is still

winter hill
my eager sled
chill wind's entrancing bite

too big, too small
too short, too long
reality never fits

winter thaw
the downcast
snowman

deep winter night
I speak a prayer
for dark-illumined guidance

twilight sun
on snow-crowned roofs
winter's chill artistry

bouncing hail
winter's
icy spit

pain framing delight

winter gale
thought after thought
after thought

serenity now!

or maybe

some other time?

death approaching

door you locked

his skeleton key

the automaticity of fear

finches fled, neighbors quelled

the stillness

of winter backyards

one step forward
one step back
his shy heart

wind-born snow
the many angles
of descent

no desire

for reputation

poet's peace

marching
in his life's parade
of thought

all the rainbows
I will miss
unhappy death bed

eager hounds

of winter drifts

snow-snuffling

tranquility
of pen-to-paper
mornings

elder years
the body's
grudging service

chill winter morn

she's singing

her closed heart open

maples after rain
the sorrow
in her eyes

her joyful mien:
lucky genes
happy childhood

guilt machine

his mind

geared to blame

breathing deep
his thoughts ascend
to silence

winter eve
a distant train
blares quietude

winter peace

I accept

my season's end

all around us
stillness reigns
pay attention

drowsing through
a darkling noon
cloud therapy

his vaudeville spark

the show-train

of his life

I want, I want

I fail

at easeful presence

winter eve

my heaviest burden

me

winter thaw

a neighbor

reappears

stillness

of my body

quietude of earth

love our life

for others, seek justice

the game's been named

all his triumphs
all his honors
winter graveyard

one boy
one tricycle
winter playground

each precision
stroke of saw
compassionate arborist

afternoon moon

a different

light

winter dawn
still and silent
gray and listening

falling star
our transitory
lives

deep night
a bedside lamp
illumines thought

meteor

by air consumed

my flaring, burning life

urban freeze

bright forest gleam

of inconvenient ice

when in my life

did snowfall switch

from beauty to nuisance?

idiot winter

blowing, snarling

season malcontent

all thing pass away

I embrace

this winter morning

deep winter night
I, calm, suspend
self-judgment

frost and ice

companion

winter waters

sibilance

of drifting snow

she listens beyond thought

winter gray
the melancholy
of clouds

winter sun
he adjusts his mind
toward hope

winter stars
the dominion
of grace

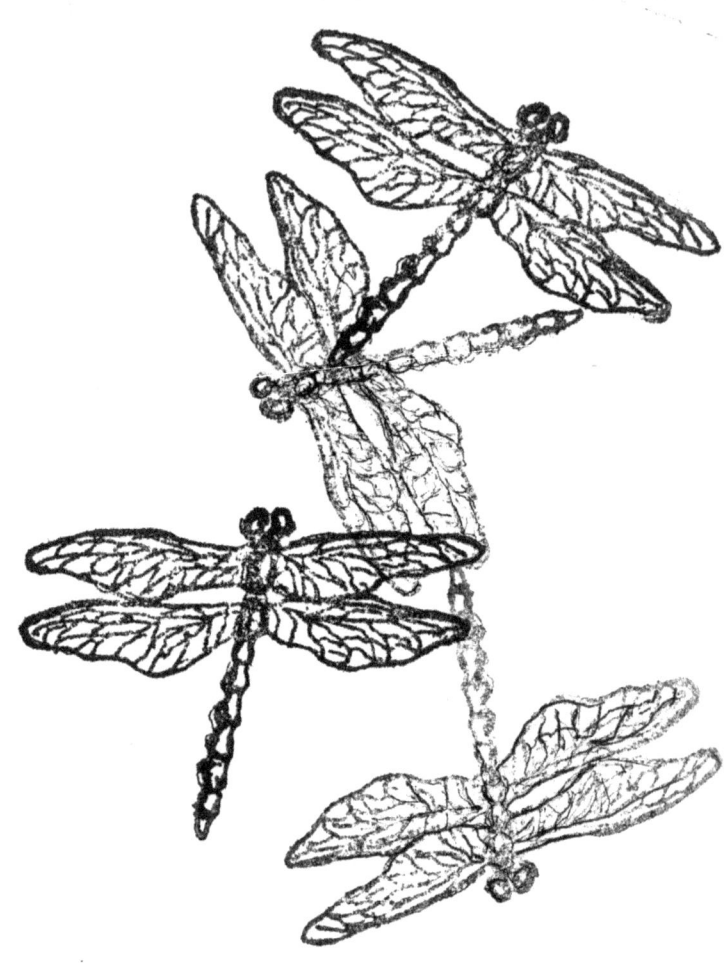

winging, scuttling
marching, leaping
merry insect spring

Fred Andrle is the author of several collections of poetry, including *Love Life* (XOXOX Press, 2008), *What Counts* (XOXOX Press, 2012), *Rocking in the Cradle of the Moment* (XOXOX Press, 2019), and *every instant offering grace* (11th Hour Press, 2021).

For more than twenty years, Fred served as executive producer and host of the public affairs talk show "Open Line" on WOSU public radio in Columbus, Ohio.

You can read more of Fred's poetry at his website: fredandrle.com

Thanks to my fellow House of Toast Poets MJ Abell, Charlene Fix, Linda Fuller-Smith, Jerry Roscoe and Jacquelin Smith for their helpful suggestions and encouragement.

Some of the haiku/senryu in this collection appeared previously in *Presence, Frogpond, Modern Haiku, Akitsu Quarterly, bottle rockets, Chrysanthemum, Failed Haiku,* Haiku Foundation *Per Diem, hedgerow,* and *World Haiku Review*.

www.ingramcontent.com/pod-product-compliance
Lightning Source LLC
Chambersburg PA
CBHW041137110526
44590CB00027B/4053